courage

INSPIRATIONAL QUOTATIONS

Whatever we do, whoever we are, we all value courage.

The words and images in this book are from many

parts of the world and different kinds of people.

Together, they indicate something of the nature of

courage and how it may be developed.

$\mathcal{B}$e of good courage. All is before you and time passed in the difficult is never lost.

RAINER MARIA RILKE

If we are intended for great ends, we are called to great hazards.

JOHN HENRY, CARDINAL NEWMAN

We learn courageous action by going forward whenever fear urges us back.

DAVID SEABURY

One doesn't discover new lands without consenting

to lose sight of the shore for a very long time.

ANDRÉ GIDE

I am not discouraged, because every wrong attempt discarded is another step forward.

THOMAS EDISON

*O*nly those who hate

to fail miserably can

achieve greatly.

ROBERT F. KENNEDY

*C*ourage is like love; it must have hope to nourish it.

NAPOLEON BONAPARTE

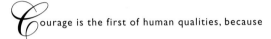ourage is the first of human qualities, because

it is the quality that guarantees all others.

SIR WINSTON CHURCHILL

*W*e have nothing to fear but fear itself.

FRANKLIN ROOSEVELT

*W*hatever you can do, or dream

you can do, begin it. Boldness has

power, magic and genius in it.

JOHANN WOLFGANG VON GOETHE

When you get into a tight place

and everything goes against you,

till it seems as though you could

not hang on a minute longer,

never give up then, for that is

just the place and time that the

tide will turn.

HARRIET BEECHER STOWE

You must do the thing you

think you cannot do.

ELEANOR ROOSEVELT

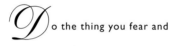o the thing you fear and

the death of fear is certain.

MARK TWAIN

Far better it is to dare mighty things, to win

glorious triumphs even though checkered by failure,

than to rank with those poor spirits who neither

enjoy nor suffer much because they live in the grey

twilight that knows neither victory nor defeat.

THEODORE ROOSEVELT

$\mathcal{W}$henever you see a successful

business, someone once made a

courageous decision.

PETER DRUCKER

*O*pportunity does not come to those who wait.

It is captured by those who attack.

GENERAL DOUGLAS MACARTHUR

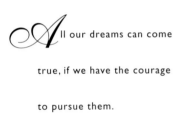ll our dreams can come

true, if we have the courage

to pursue them.

WALT DISNEY

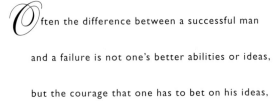

*O*ften the difference between a successful man

and a failure is not one's better abilities or ideas,

but the courage that one has to bet on his ideas,

to take a calculated risk and to act.

MAXWELL MALTZ

*W*hat is more mortifying than to feel that you have missed the

plum for want of courage to shake the tree?

LOGAN PEARSALL SMITH

$\mathcal{K}$eep your fears to yourself, but share your courage with others.

ROBERT LOUIS STEVENSON

*I*t is when people hurt you

badly that you move forward.

Life is about going on, and not

giving up when you're put down.

GEORGE DAVIS

The fishermen know that the

sea is dangerous and storm terrible,

but they never found these dangers

sufficient reason for remaining ashore.

VINCENT VAN GOGH

*I*t is a blessed thing that in every age someone

has had individuality enough and courage enough

to stand by his own conviction.

ROBERT G. INGERSOLL

ourage is not the absence of fear,

it is the control of fear.

RUDYARD KIPLING

$\mathcal{M}$any of our fears are

tissue-paper thin, and a

single courageous step

would carry us clear

through them.

JULIA FLETCHER CARNEY

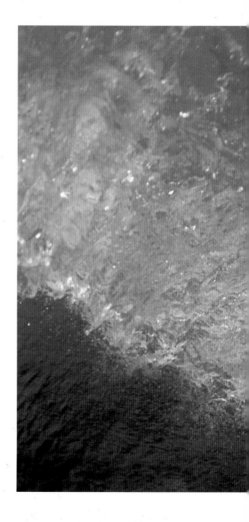

It is courage the world

needs, not infallibility...

courage is always the

surest wisdom.

SIR WILFRED GRENFELL

ur doubts are traitors, and

make us lose the good we oft

might win by fearing to attempt.

WILLIAM SHAKESPEARE

$\mathcal{L}$ife is either a daring

adventure or nothing.

HELEN KELLER

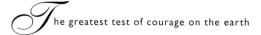

*T*he greatest test of courage on the earth

is to bear defeat without losing heart.

ROBERT G. INGERSOLL

$\mathscr{Y}$ou gain strength, courage and

confidence by every experience

in which you really stop to look

fear in the face.

ELEANOR ROOSEVELT

What would life be if we had no courage to attempt anything?

VINCENT VAN GOGH

*T*he only service a friend can really render

is to keep up your courage by holding up to you

a mirror in which you can see a noble image of yourself.

GEORGE BERNARD SHAW

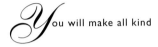ou will make all kind

of mistakes but as long as

you are generous and true,

and also fierce, you cannot

hurt the world or even

seriously disturb her.

SIR WINSTON CHURCHILL

Published in England by

FOUR SEASONS
PUBLISHING

16 Orchard Rise, Kingston upon Thames, Surrey, KT2 7EY

Designed in association with
THE BRIDGEWATER BOOK COMPANY

Printed in Singapore

Text selected by Pauline Barrett

The publishers would like to thank Gettyone Stone Picture Library the use of pictures.